642
THINGS TO DRAW

CHRONICLE BOOKS
SAN FRANCISCO

ISBN: 978-0-8118-7644-5

Manufactured in China.

Design by Eloise Leigh

30 29 28 27 26 25

Chronicle Books LLC
680 Second Street
San Francisco, California 94107

www.chroniclebooks.com

a rolling pin

a hammock

an anchor

a skunk

a desk chair

Van Gogh's ear

a sandwich

a string quartet

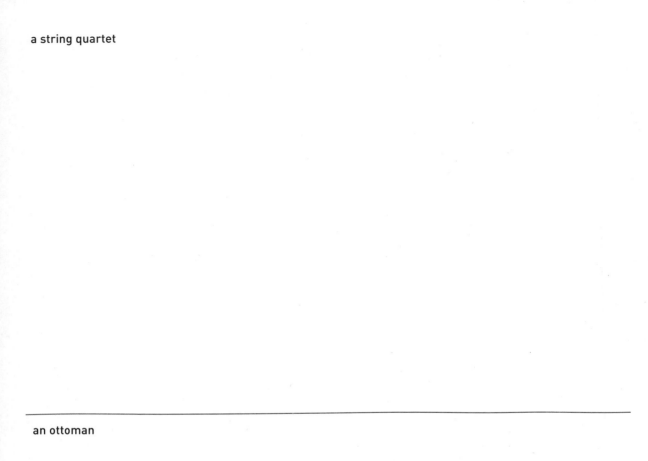

an ottoman

a bottle opener

a fire escape

luminescent plankton

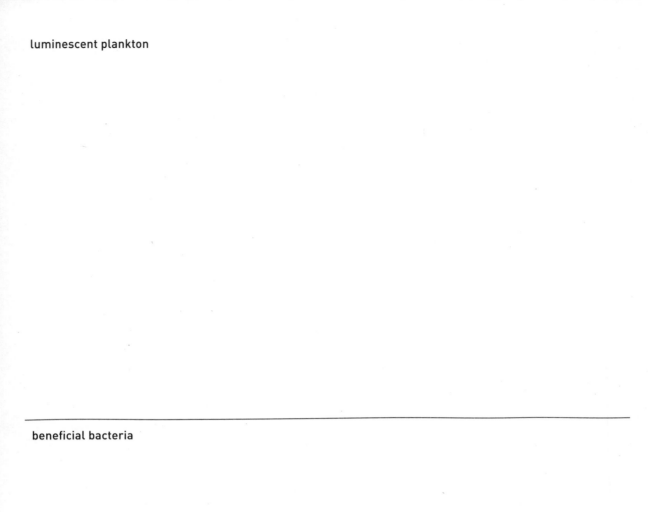

beneficial bacteria

a cabin

mushrooms

shrubbery

Bob Marley

a full house

bubbles

fangs

a pickle

an ironing board

a dolphin

a paper clip

a trumpet

a burrito

tube socks | a crayon

a roller coaster

a mosquito

fruit cocktail

a peg leg

a spigot

a balloon

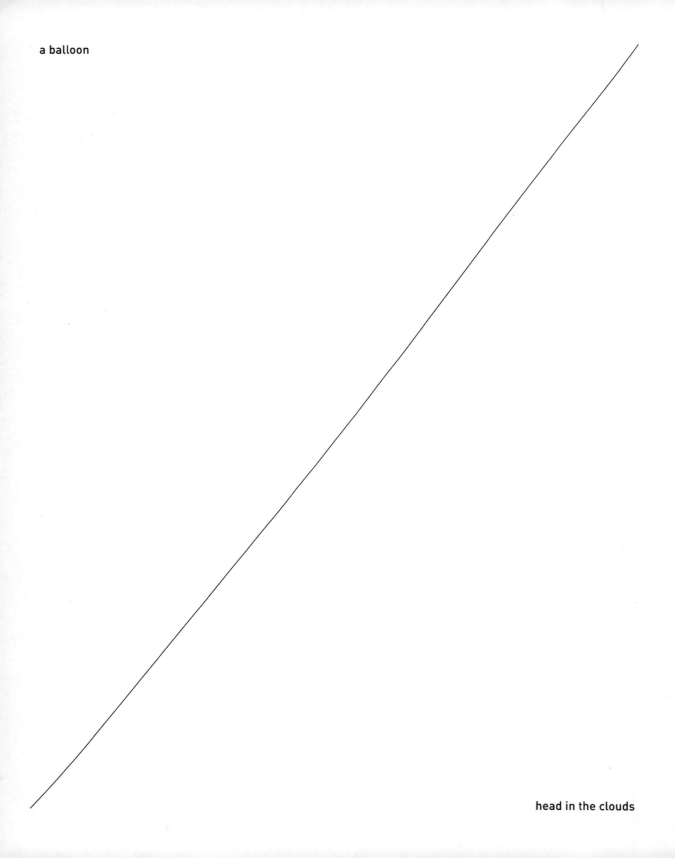

head in the clouds

a knot

an old key

a submarine

a tulip

a gold medal

synchronized swimmers

a juice box

a jar full of pennies

a bag of hammers

jelly beans

a sundial

a crystal ball

a synthesizer

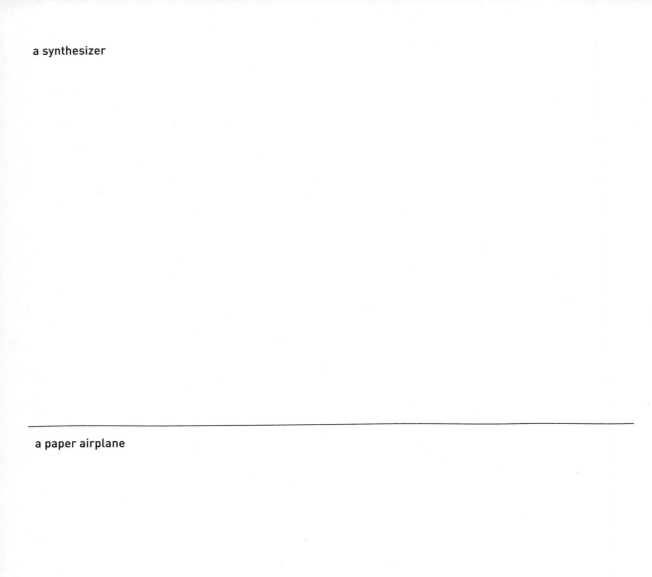

a paper airplane

a water tower

a surfboard

New Jersey

Fiji

a layer cake

a panda

a mime

Charlie Chaplin

a penguin

a seagull | David Bowie

a sensitive cowboy | a leopard

an anatomy chart

a tree limb

a ship in a bottle

a mouth

brass knuckles

an ear of corn

a mirage

smoke

mold

a rainbow

a dollar bill

a bone

a glass of milk

a teapot

weeds

dance steps

a turkey leg

a pencil

a picket fence

a Tiffany lamp | the Empire State Building

a stalagmite

a stalactite

a kiss

a ladybug

a helmet

a paw print

a T-shirt

a cinder block

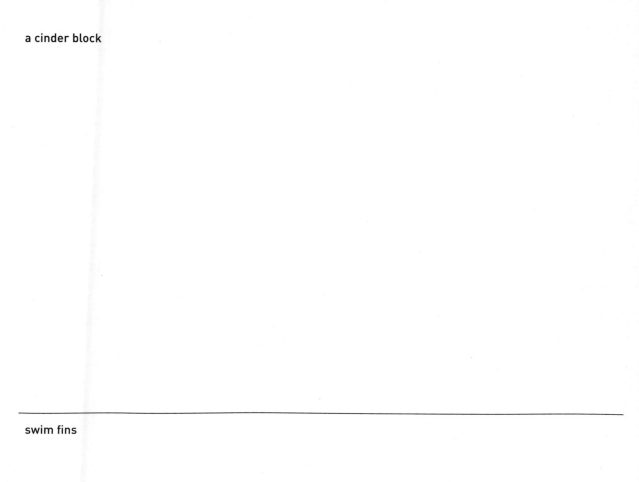

swim fins

a ripe banana

a barbell

a tennis racket

a spiral staircase

a ponytail

a campfire

a squirrel

a thumb

a book

girlish laughter

tangled ribbons

noodles

best friends

bunting

an accordion

a log

a melting candle

a phone booth

a geode

dice

ointment

a bucket

a digital watch

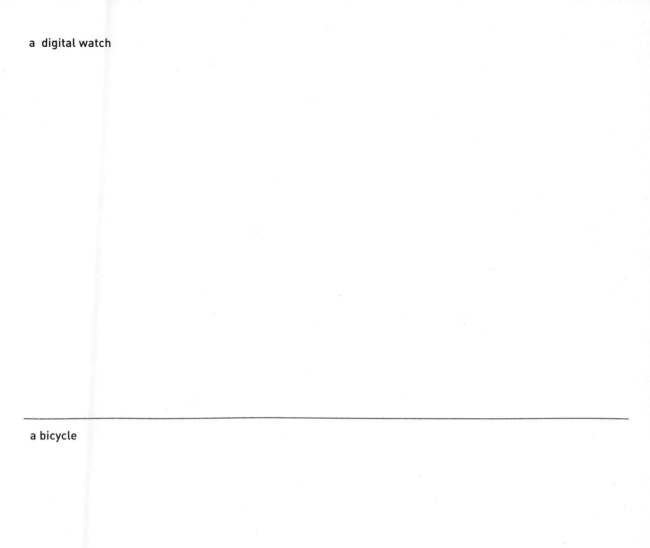

a bicycle

a cassette tape

---

a library card

a corn dog with mustard

mittens

a pocket

a bunch of grapes

a vending machine

a typewriter

a flamingo

a kebab

shelves

a necklace

a dirty rag

a scallion pancake

a time machine

a Tyrannosaurus rex

a music box

a candelabra

a quarter

a bulldog

a fairy

a ball of yarn

a haircut

an electric guitar | confetti

a pair of scissors

a bandage

a watermelon

bacon

a newsboy cap

a seed pod

a board game

daffodils

an onion

a slinky

a keychain

a sand castle

leftovers

a ghost

a vampire

a football

a lightbulb

a horseshoe

a pug

a helicopter

a warthog

a basket

a skateboard

sea spray

seaweed

an umbrella | a Christmas tree

a hamburger

sunglasses

a seal

twenty thousand leagues under the sea

a shooting star

handprints

a rotary phone

a top hat

a turtle

a baseball

an airplane

a microphone

a saxophone | an ice cream cone

a marble

a weathervane

a lunchbox

a pound

a trolley car

cat whiskers

a cleaver

a Quonset hut

a treasure chest

binoculars

a pumpkin

a chalkboard

stiletto heels

a crowd

a pile of tires | a zombie

french fries

a caterpillar

a watering can

a cactus

coral

---

playing cards

a celebration

a constellation

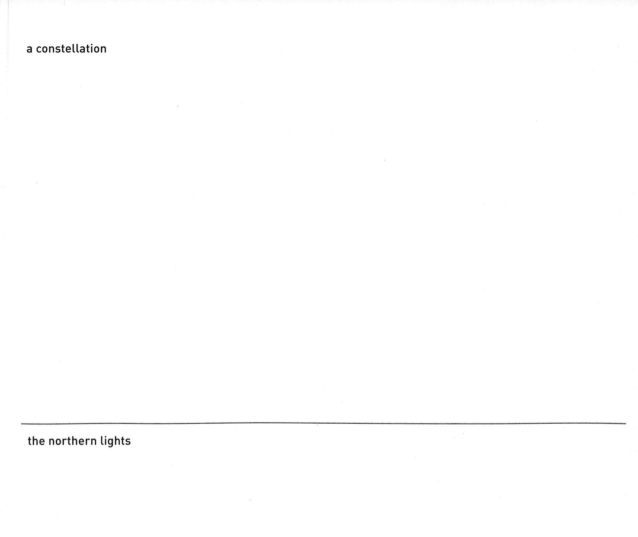

the northern lights

bonbons

a wink

an inchworm

a knife

a kite

the Olympics

a box of tissues

a balloon animal

a spiral-bound notebook

a salt shaker

a bearded lady

a wrinkle

a box of kittens

a slug

a shadow

a winter hat

a puzzle

a diving board

a spoon

a cuttlefish

rain

eyelashes

a diaper

a bottle cap

Queen Victoria

a bird feeder

a baguette | a ladder

a parade

running shoes

bowling shoes

an apple tree

---

a storm

a fan

a princess crown

broccoli

a sarcophagus

a stick of butter

a sled

a flattop

a bonnet

a baseball glove

Elvis

a rubber duck

a milk carton

a diamond ring

feelings

Mom

Dad

a drunken sailor

a police officer

snowshoes | a necktie

a bowler hat

a unicycle

a frog

a paper coffee cup

a waterslide

spilled milk

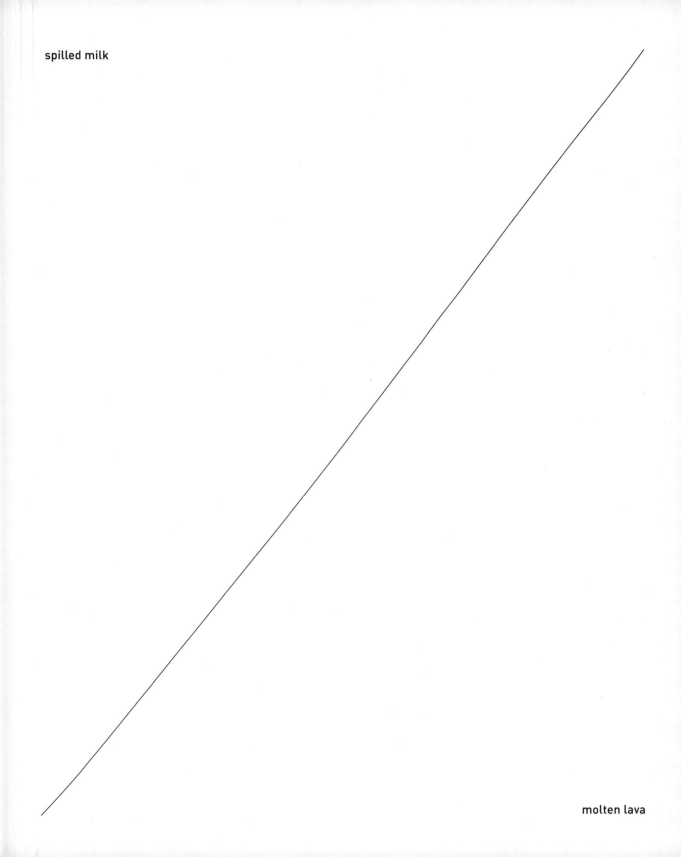

molten lava

a spaceship

a sound wave

clogs

an open/closed sign

the view from an airplane window

knitting needles

the Little Prince

a box of cereal

toes

chips and dip

a newt

a moustache

a face full of character

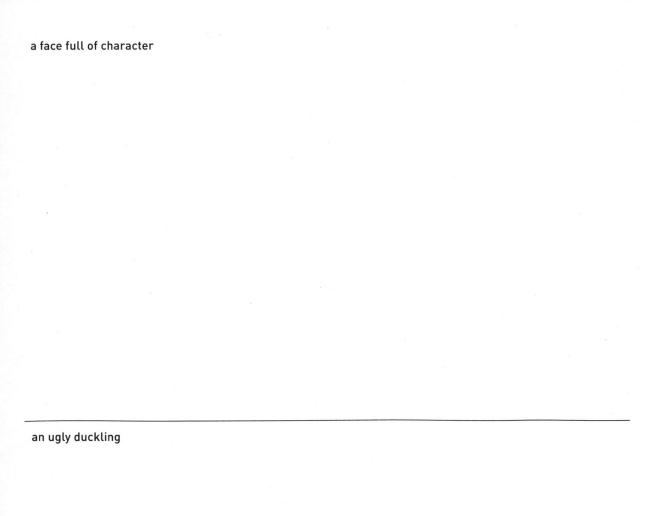

an ugly duckling

a laser

the Leaning Tower of Pisa

scrambled eggs

a caribou

an eyeball

a chimney

a drum kit

a battleship

whirling dervishes

a fashion model | fancy pants

hot springs

steak and potatoes

a spool of thread

the wild blue yonder

a rabbit

a boom box

a bird's nest

a power tool

a butterfly

toast

a computer

an eye patch

a crab apple

a golf ball

cutlery

a Q-tip

an office park

a sock monkey

a clock tower

a snorkel

a scorpion

a sardine tin

a secret door

a compound fracture

---

a bookstore

---

dumplings

a bowl of pudding

a director's chair

a beetle

a water jug

your least favorite food

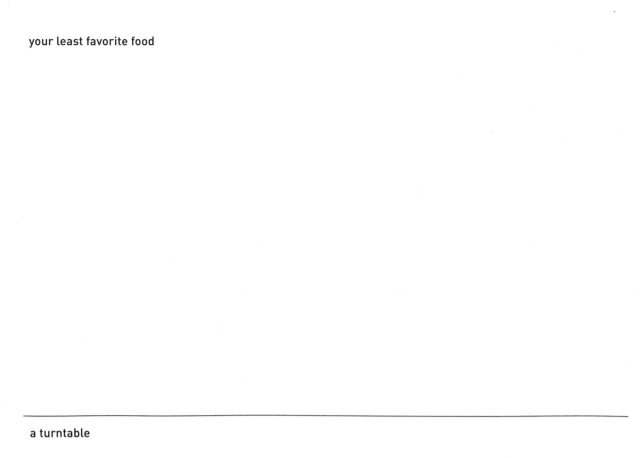

a turntable

a wheel of fortune

a fainting goat

a dumpster

a parasite | lipstick

an oasis

a frying pan

potato salad

buttons

a lumberjack

an artichoke

a flower

a teacup

a map

a moose

a palm tree

a bear family

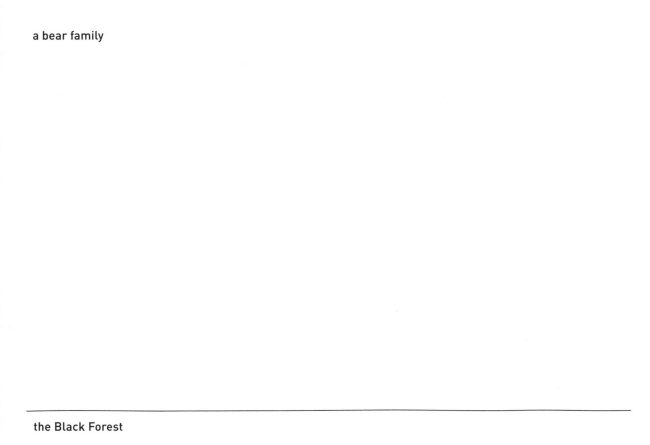

the Black Forest

a keyboard

an anteater

a comet

Noah's ark

popcorn

mac and cheese

the moon

an apron

an antelope

petroleum jelly

an uneventful street

bricks

a wormhole

perfume

a giraffe

a chainsaw

cotton candy

a sidewalk

a sailboat

---

a fjord

a brain

Saturn

a ticket

a barrel of monkeys

a real estate agent

tears

first love

middle school

a lock

a tongue

Puget Sound

peanut butter

a cranky old man

roller skates

a pillow

a gnome

a bully

a puppet

an opera singer

alphabet soup

a lollipop

contrails

a hanger

a motel

a string of DNA

a squid

a stick of gum

a ballpoint pen

a cornucopia

a gravestone

teeth

icicles

a snout | a cabbage patch

an inner tube | an elephant

an Egyptian pyramid

a narwhal

a swimming pool

fresh air

---

an iceberg

a cello

a stoplight

a dream

a nightmare

a fire truck

---

a tea bag

---

tiny ballerinas

an electrical outlet

a game-show host

a technological diagram

footprints

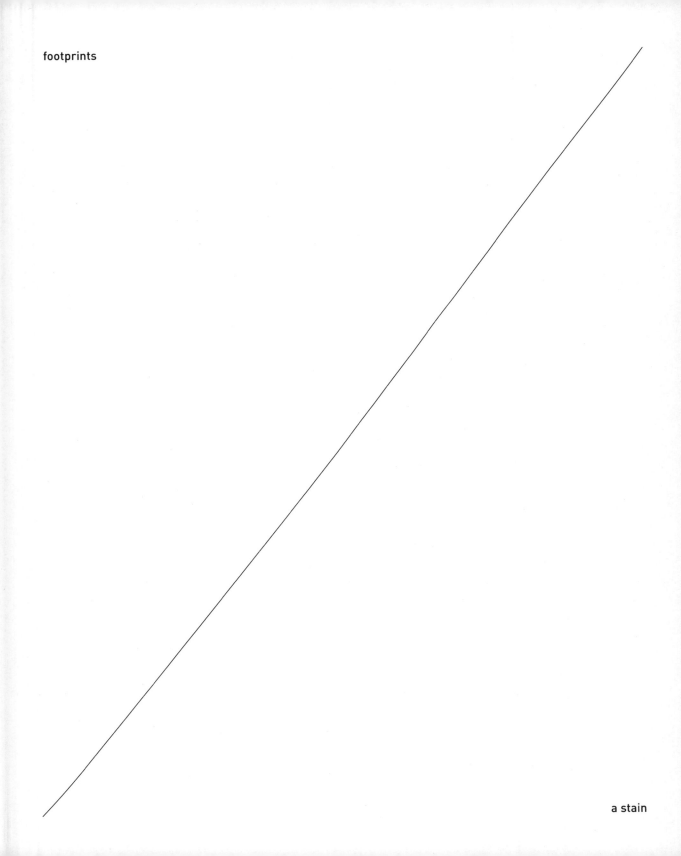

a stain

unmentionables

a porcupine

bugs

a thumbtack

a cupcake

a steak

a pirate flag

a bowling pin | a loading crane

a jungle

a tube of toothpaste

a turnip

a trailer

an orb

a long-playing record

a centaur

Mount Rushmore

a labyrinth

your pinky finger

a wooly mammoth

a boss

an ashtray

a walnut

a burlap sack

mismatched earrings

freckles

a chessboard

a tetherball

root beer

dimples

---

a poodle

---

a box car

a church | an architect

nails | a cowbell

a bus stop

leisure wear

a huge gold frame

a whisper

a scream

a jellyfish

a skeleton

a toaster

a hummingbird

a condiment

a safety pin

a garden

lucky charms

a partner in crime

the man in the moon

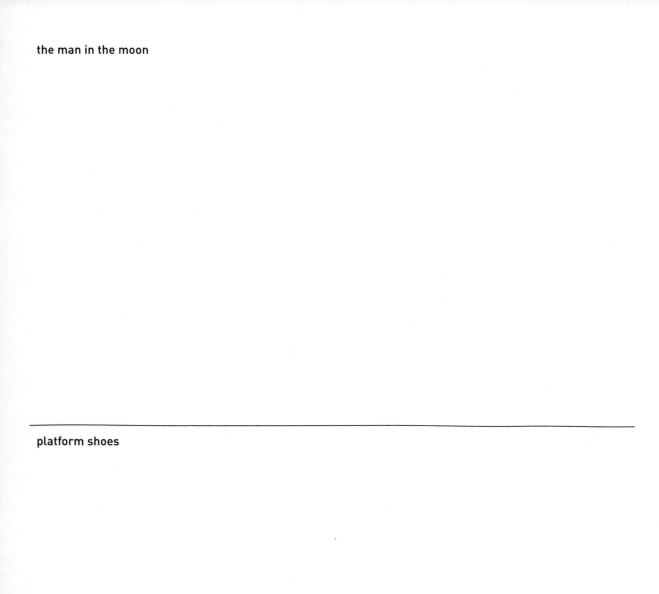

platform shoes

a quilt

a doily

vitamins

a belt buckle

a container ship

a scoundrel | crutches

a dandy

a waterfall

a circus

a troll

---

a deserted island

an owl

a beaker

a jumper

a pearl

a broken toy

a seashell

a feathered hat

an amoeba

---

tie-dye

a bobsledder

a houseboat

a gourd

a saint

a playsuit

an orphan

a bow and arrow

a pinecone

curtains

a wallet

a messenger bag

shrimp cocktail

an eggbeater

a sheep

a blackberry bush

spats

a carrot top   **a freezer**

a Scottie dog

a pineapple upside-down cake

a telescope

a mystery box

a bird in the hand

a horse and carriage

skee ball

a razor blade

a goldfish

a recycling bin

a road

windows

an egg

a birdhouse

a sweatband

a strawberry

sushi

a hippo

a prism

a sense of humor

pie à la mode

a dragonfly

a tractor

behind the scenes

2 x 4s

a lava lamp

a harmonica

a ruler

Virginia Woolf   a windmill plateaus

a crash-test dummy

a starfish

rain boots

a shoulder shrug

a pomegranate

a Beatles song

a hobo   a portal

a wheelbarrow

a three-toed sloth

a box of fried chicken

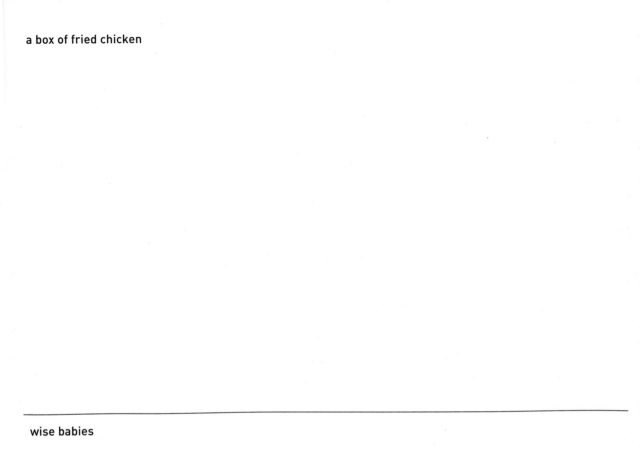

wise babies

the Abominable Snow Man

cookies

prescription medication

capes

a tarantula

a can of beans

a sand dollar

a bee

a parasol

an ink pot

a sippy cup

maple syrup

a video game

tectonic plates

a beach

a wedding dress | a spelunker

a calculator

a baby monster

a transportation system

an invitation

an oven

a train

a heart

a movie star

a spiderweb

an igloo

presidential pets

paisley

a grandma

lightning

wind

a tuxedo

a mayonnaise jar

a lemon meringue pie

a sea urchin

a canyon

a cave

a concert

a viper

a phonograph

a bow

a convertible

ski slopes | a mummy

broken glass

a bed

a bar of music

polka dots

woodgrain

plaid

zigzag

a tacky rug

a plastic bag

a muffin tin

a sweater

a tuba

yourself